Original title:
The Sails of Social Bonds

Copyright © 2024 Swan Charm

Author: Lan Donne
ISBN HARDBACK: 978-9916-86-695-5
ISBN PAPERBACK: 978-9916-86-696-2
ISBN EBOOK: 978-9916-86-697-9

Friendship Across the Sea

Waves that dance, a bond so bright,
Two hearts linked, by day and night.
Though oceans wide, we share the same,
In laughter's echo, we play the game.

Letters float on salty air,
Stories shared, without a care.
Friendships forged on distant shores,
In every heartbeat, friendship soars.

Beyond the Tempest

Storm clouds gather, skies turn gray,
Yet hope shines through, a guiding ray.
Together we stand, against the gale,
Each whisper of courage, we prevail.

The winds may howl, but we won't bend,
Side by side, a hand to lend.
In the darkest nights, our light won't fade,
For in our hearts, true strength is made.

Anchored in Trust

In silent depths, our secrets lie,
An anchor strong, it won't run dry.
Through shifting tides, our bond holds tight,
Trust forged in shadows, shines so bright.

When doubts arise, we'll face the storm,
In unity's embrace, we feel warm.
With every challenge, we shall thrive,
Together, dear friend, we come alive.

Swells of Unity

Like the ocean, vast and free,
Our voices rise in harmony.
Each swell brings forth a shared refrain,
Together we dance, in joy, in pain.

From every shore, we reach and blend,
In this vast sea, you're my best friend.
With hearts as one, we'll brave the tide,
In unity's warmth, we shall abide.

Sail in the Same Direction

With sails unfurled we chart our way,
Together we rise, in light of day.
The winds of hope, they guide our helm,
In unity strong, we claim our realm.

Through stormy seas we face the night,
With hearts aligned, we find our light.
Each wave we conquer makes us bold,
In shared dreams, our story unfolds.

Compass of Connections

A compass spins, it finds its true,
Amidst the stars, I'm lost in you.
With every bond, a guiding star,
In friendship's light, we've come so far.

Through tangled paths our spirits weave,
In every glance, we dare to believe.
With laughter shared and hands held tight,
We navigate through day and night.

Journeying in Unity

Together we walk, side by side,
In harmony's dance, we take our stride.
With every step, we pave the way,
In trust and love, we choose to stay.

The road may twist, it may turn,
But in our hearts, we feel the burn.
Of purpose shared and dreams in sight,
We journey forth into the light.

Shores of Support

Upon the shores where friendships grow,
In gentle waves, our courage flows.
With every tide, we lift each other,
In strength united, we find our mother.

Through changing sands, we plant our feet,
With open arms, our hearts we greet.
In bonds of trust, we make our stand,
Together as one, we face the land.

Sailing the Sea of Support

With sails unfurled, we drift along,
Through waves of hope, we sing our song.
In storms we find the strength to stand,
Together we navigate this land.

Each gust a whisper, a guiding hand,
In laughter and silence, we make our stand.
The horizon's glow, our dreams ignite,
In the sea of support, we find our light.

Bonds of Gossamer Light

In threads so fine, our spirits weave,
With gentle touch, we learn to believe.
Each moment shared, a shimmering tie,
In the tapestry of life, we soar high.

Through laughter's echo, and sorrows mild,
Together we bloom, like a cherished child.
In the dance of time, our hearts unite,
We shine like stars, in bonds of light.

Voyage of Understanding

With every wave, we learn and grow,
In the depths of silence, truths we sow.
The compass of kindness guides our way,
In the voyage of understanding, we stay.

Through storms of doubt, we find our course,
With open hearts, we tap the source.
In shared reflections, wisdom gleams,
Together we chase, our vivid dreams.

Shared Journeys

On open roads, our paths align,
With laughter loud, our spirits shine.
In every turn, a story told,
In shared journeys, our hearts unfold.

Through mountains high and valleys deep,
In echoes of memories, treasures we keep.
Together we wander, hand in hand,
In the tapestry of travels, we stand.

Cresting the Waves of Connection

In the silence, we find our voice,
A whisper shared, a silent choice.
Through stormy seas, our hearts align,
Together we weave a bond divine.

Bridges built on trust and grace,
We navigate this vast open space.
With every crest, our spirits rise,
In connection's glow, we touch the skies.

Each pulse a promise, light and clear,
In every heartbeat, I hold you near.
As tides may shift, we hold on tight,
In shared reflections, we find our light.

Beacons of Belonging

Amidst the shadows, we stand tall,
With open arms, we welcome all.
Together forging paths of hope,
In laughter's echo, we learn to cope.

Our voices blend in harmony sweet,
In every story, our lives meet.
A circle drawn with hearts aglow,
In belonging's warmth, our spirits grow.

One gentle smile, a touch, a sign,
In this vast world, your hand in mine.
We shine as beacons, bright and true,
In every heartbeat, I see you.

Together We Set Sail

With sails unfurled, we catch the breeze,
In friendship forged, our souls find ease.
The horizon calls, adventure awaits,
With courage strong, we open gates.

Each wave a rhythm, a song untold,
In the journey, our dreams unfold.
Facing the storms, we will not falter,
In unity's strength, our fears we alter.

The compass pointed to the stars,
Together, no distance feels too far.
Our hearts the anchors, deep and wide,
In this vast ocean, you're by my side.

Journeying Through Lighthouses

Through misty veils, we find our way,
Guided by light that will not sway.
With every beacon, a tale unfolds,
In the warmth of kindness, our hearts are bold.

The waves may crash, the winds may roar,
But side by side, we'll brave the shore.
Each lighthouse shines, a guiding friend,
In the darkest nights, it will defend.

We chart our course on shores unknown,
In love's embrace, we've truly grown.
Together we journey, hand in hand,
In the glow of lighthouses, we make our stand.

Discovering Depths Together

In twilight's glow, we dive so deep,
Exploring wonders that secrets keep.
Hand in hand, we wander down,
In the silence, lost, we drown.

Beneath the waves, the colors bloom,
With every heartbeat, we consume.
The world in whispers unfolds wide,
In shared breaths, we do not hide.

Stories linger in the tide,
As we drift on this gentle ride.
Every ripple tells our tale,
In the sea, our hearts unveil.

Together we rise, together we fall,
Boundless depths, we heed the call.
In the ocean's embrace, we find,
A treasure rare, two souls aligned.

Paddling Through Life's Waters

With every stroke, we cut the stream,
In the sunlight, we chase our dream.
Together we glide, side by side,
In the rhythm, we take our stride.

Waves may crash and winds may roar,
But united, we seek to explore.
The current's pull may twist and bend,
Yet in each bend, new paths we send.

Life's tempests may test our might,
But in the journey, we find our light.
With laughter shared and burdens light,
Our hearts dance as day turns to night.

Through valleys low and peaks so tall,
Together we conquer, together we fall.
With paddle in hand, our spirits soar,
In every moment, we find our core.

The North Star of Connection

In the night sky, a beacon gleams,
A guiding light for all our dreams.
Through storms we sail, on course we steer,
With trust as our anchor, we persevere.

Each twinkling star a story told,
Of laughter shared and hands to hold.
Through quiet moments, we align,
In the universe, our hearts entwine.

Celestial dances, our souls embrace,
In the cosmic rhythm, we find our place.
Together we navigate the night,
Finding solace in each other's light.

When shadows loom and fears arise,
We look up high to the starlit skies.
With every glance, our hearts we share,
In the vastness, a love so rare.

Sailing with Kindness

With gentle winds and sails unfurled,
We journey forth into the world.
In kindness, we find our way,
A compass set for brighter days.

Each wave we meet is softened sweet,
With hearts open, our souls greet.
Through storms that rise, we remain calm,
In every challenge, find the balm.

The horizon calls, a vision clear,
With every cheer, we draw near.
In unity, our hopes align,
As we chart paths where dreams combine.

The sea reflects our shades of grace,
In every smile, take your place.
With kindness leading, we embark,
Through tranquil waters, we leave our mark.

Whispers on the Water

Gentle ripples kiss the shore,
Secrets linger, long and low.
Moonlit paths, they softly glow,
Carries dreams where silence swore.

Breezes hum a tender tune,
Softly swaying dreams in flight.
Stars above, a scattered boon,
Guide the heart through velvet night.

Each reflection tells a tale,
Of hopes born in twilight's gleam.
Carried by the tides, we sail,
Trusting whispers of the stream.

Silken threads of night entwined,
Nature speaks in hushed respect.
In this moment, peace we find,
Dance of water, pure, perfect.

So let the currents call your name,
Let them wash away your fears.
In the flow, we're all the same,
Whispers echo through the years.

Threads of Connection

In the fabric of our days,
Woven deep, our stories blend.
Every glance, a subtle phrase,
Threads of connection never end.

Through laughter's bright and dancing light,
And shadows where our sorrows lie.
Together we ignite the night,
In memories that never die.

Each whisper shared, a bond refined,
Sewn with love through every tear.
As seasons shift and hearts align,
Cosmic ties, so strong and clear.

Weaving dreams with colors bold,
In the tapestry we make.
With every thread, our truths unfold,
In every promise, love's awake.

So here we stand, hand in hand,
Our spirits dance, our fears release.
In this woven, sacred land,
Threads of connection, find their peace.

Anchored Hearts

In the harbor of our souls,
Love's a vessel, strong and true.
Through storms that test and take their tolls,
Anchored hearts, we will renew.

Each sunset paints the sky with grace,
And every dawn brings hope anew.
In the calm, we share our space,
Treasured moments, always few.

Together, through the waves we ride,
With courage cast in every sigh.
In every ebb, we will abide,
Boundless love that cannot die.

Though tides may pull, and winds may shift,
We find our strength in gentle trust.
In love's embrace, our souls uplift,
Anchored hearts, we know we must.

For in this journey, hand in hand,
We weather life, both fierce and shy.
Like ships that sail on golden sand,
Anchored hearts will always fly.

Beyond the Horizon's Embrace

As dawn unfolds its tender light,
We chase the dreams that beckon near.
Beyond the horizon's gentle sight,
Adventures wait, both bright and clear.

With every step, the world expands,
New paths awake, new tales unfurl.
Together now, let fate command,
In every moment, let's explore.

Though shadows linger, fears arise,
In courage found, we take our stand.
With open hearts and open eyes,
Beyond the waves, we make our plans.

Dreams like kites, they soar and glide,
With hope our sail, we'll never tire.
In unison, our souls will bide,
Chasing horizons, always higher.

So here we journey, side by side,
Embracing all that time bestows.
Beyond the horizon, wide and wide,
Our love will grow, and forever flow.

Captained by Kindness

In the harbor of our hearts,
Kindness casts her gentle sail,
Riding waves of empathy,
Together we set our trail.

With every turn and swell,
Compassion guides our way,
Through storms that may arise,
We treasure each shared day.

A lighthouse bright and true,
Hope shines in the distance,
Hand in hand we journey forth,
Embracing each existence.

With laughter as our compass,
And love that never dims,
We chart a course so sweet,
A rhythm in our hymns.

As we sail through life's vast sea,
Captained by kindness' hand,
We find in every wave,
A place where dreams expand.

Navigating Life Together

In a world that shifts and sways,
We find our way, hand in hand,
With laughter as our guide,
And trust, our steadfast band.

Through tangled paths we wander,
Each step a dance of grace,
With love, we map our journey,
Finding joy in every place.

When shadows seem to linger,
And doubts begin to climb,
We lift each other higher,
In rhythm, keeping time.

With every twist and turn,
We learn to bend, not break,
In union, we discover,
The strength that we can make.

Navigating life together,
With hearts all intertwined,
We paint the world in color,
With every dream aligned.

Drift of Affection

On a gentle breeze, we sway,
Like leaves in tender flight,
In the silence of the night,
Our hearts find pure delight.

With whispers soft as feathers,
Affection's tender glow,
We drift on waves of comfort,
In trust, we surely flow.

A dance beneath the moonlight,
Where shadows gently play,
With every glance exchanged,
Our worries fade away.

Floating on this river,
Of love and sweet embrace,
In the drift of affection,
We find our sacred space.

Every moment cherished,
Like ripples in a stream,
In the drift of affection,
We nurture every dream.

Tranquil Waters of Friendship

In tranquil waters, we sail,
Friendship guides our way,
With every shared adventure,
We brighten up the day.

Amidst the gentle currents,
We anchor side by side,
In the laughter and the silence,
Our hearts forever tied.

Through every stormy moment,
We'll weather tempests bold,
In the quiet of together,
A warmth that won't grow old.

With every wave we conquer,
And every path we roam,
In the tranquil waters,
We always call it home.

Together we are stronger,
A bond that's ever true,
In tranquil waters of friendship,
My soul finds peace in you.

Shared Horizons

Beneath the vast and open sky,
We chase our dreams, you and I.
With every step, our spirits rise,
Together, we embrace the skies.

Paths entwined, we laugh and roam,
In every heart, we find a home.
The world expands with shared delight,
As day turns softly into night.

Hand in hand, we forge ahead,
In whispered tales, our hopes are fed.
With every sunrise, fears depart,
In unity, we start anew.

Memories painted in hues of gold,
Inspiring stories yet untold.
With you beside, there's strength in numbers,
A bond that wakes from endless slumbers.

Horizons blend in shades so bright,
In every shadow, we ignite.
Through shared horizons, we will strive,
Together, forever, we'll arrive.

The Catch of Companionship

On the shore where waves do dance,
We cast our nets with hopeful chance.
The tides may shift, but here we stay,
With every catch, we find our way.

Together, we sail the stormy seas,
Laughing under the whispering breeze.
In every wave, a secret shared,
In the depths, our souls laid bare.

The flicker of light on water's face,
Reminds us of our sacred space.
In the catch of hearts, we find our peace,
A bond that shall never cease.

With every cast, we weave a tale,
From every triumph, we shall sail.
Through fin and scale, through joy and pain,
Companionship, our sweetest gain.

As night descends, the stars align,
In your laughter, I find the divine.
The catch of companionship shines bright,
Guiding us safely through the night.

Woven into the Wind

In whispers soft, the breezes call,
By tangled roots, we rise and fall.
Each thread of air pulls us along,
In nature's heart, we find our song.

As leaves embrace the golden rays,
We dance through ephemeral days.
Woven tightly, our spirits blend,
In every gust, we find a friend.

The wind, a painter of the scene,
With colors vibrant, bright, and keen.
In every rustle, stories live,
A tapestry of love to give.

Through valleys deep and mountains high,
We ride the currents, you and I.
Forever carried on the breeze,
In harmony with ancient trees.

Woven into the skies so wide,
In nature's arms, we take our stride.
Together, we soar, our spirits free,
In the wind's embrace, just you and me.

Guiding Lights on the Ocean

Stars above, they softly gleam,
Whispers of the ocean's dream.
Waves that dance in silver light,
Leading ships through endless night.

Lanterns bright on distant shores,
Calling sailors to explore.
With each beam that pierces dark,
Hope ignites a glowing spark.

In the night, a calm embrace,
Guiding hearts to find their place.
Echoes of a sailor's song,
In the tides where dreams belong.

The horizon's vast, unknown,
Yet the light can lead you home.
Every wave a tale untold,
In the night, we are bold.

Anchors drop, the journey starts,
With the stars, we'll share our hearts.
Guiding lights, you show the way,
In your glow, we find our stay.

From Dusk till Dawn

Shadows stretch as day departs,
Painting skies with tender arts.
Whispers float on evening air,
Promises beyond compare.

Stars awaken, softly lit,
In the night, the dreams we fit.
From dusk, the world begins to sigh,
In the hush, our hopes can fly.

Moonlight casts a silver glow,
Guiding paths where lovers go.
Silhouettes in quiet dance,
Finding joy in every glance.

As the clock strikes midnight's tune,
Hearts entwined beneath the moon.
Moments pass like fleeting streams,
Wrapped in soft, enchanting dreams.

With dawn's light, the night retreats,
Yet the magic still completes.
From dusk to dawn, forever sway,
In the glow of a brand new day.

Unity in the Breeze

Gentle winds that softly sway,
Bring us closer through the day.
Whispers in the rustling leaves,
Nature's song, our hearts it weaves.

From mountain peaks to ocean waves,
In each breath, the spirit braves.
Together we share the air,
In each moment, we declare.

Harmony in every gust,
In our bond, we place our trust.
United, we take to flight,
Embraced in the warmth of light.

Through the trees, a tender kiss,
In the breeze, a state of bliss.
Hand in hand, we roam the earth,
Finding joy in every worth.

As the world spins round and round,
In each heartbeat, love is found.
Unity in every breeze,
Together, we are at ease.

The Promise of a Fair Wind

In the harbor, whispers swell,
Tales of journeys we can tell.
Sails unfurl, the horizon calls,
Embracing winds, adventure befalls.

With each breeze, a promise made,
Of new paths we won't evade.
Through tempests fierce, we sail along,
Found in every heartbeat's song.

As the sun breaks through the gray,
Guided by a light that stays.
Hope is woven in the thread,
Of every seam where dreams are led.

Together we brave the unknown,
In every sea, love has grown.
With the wind as our faithful guide,
We'll conquer waves, side by side.

So let the fair winds take us high,
Through uncharted depths, we'll fly.
In the promise of the breeze,
We find courage, hearts at ease.

Unified in the Storm

Amidst the raging seas we stand,
Together, side by side, hand in hand.
The winds may howl, the shadows loom,
But in our hearts, we light the room.

With every crash of thunder's might,
We find our strength, we claim the night.
A bond unbroken, fierce and true,
Forever strong, just me and you.

As lightning strikes and chaos reigns,
We'll brave the tides, embrace the pains.
Unified by hope, we fight as one,
Our journey's path has just begun.

The storm may shake, the clouds may cry,
But we will soar, we will not die.
For in this tempest, love's our guide,
Together we face the wild tide.

So let the storm come, fierce and bold,
Together, we'll gather stories untold.
In the heart of chaos, we'll ignite
A flame of courage burning bright.

Waves of Whispered Promises

Upon the shore, where dreams collide,
The whispers ride the ebbing tide.
Each wave a vow, a gentle sound,
In depths of love, we are unbound.

The ocean speaks in rhythmic grace,
With each embrace, we find our place.
Promises dance upon the sea,
Like grains of sand, we're wild and free.

As seagulls cry and sunsets paint,
Our hopes ascend, no room for faint.
With every crest, the future gleams,
In waves of whispers, we chase our dreams.

Together we venture, hearts entwined,
With every storm, our love defined.
Through tides that shift and skies that change,
We'll ride the waves, our spirits range.

So hear the ocean's soft refrain,
In every pulse, our love's the same.
With open hearts, we sail along,
In waves of whispered promises, we're strong.

Tides of Friendship

In every season, side by side,
We navigate the changing tide.
With laughter shared and burdens light,
We find our way through day and night.

When clouds gather and shadows fall,
In tides of friendship, we stand tall.
A bond that's forged through stormy days,
Will guide us through life's winding ways.

With every wave that ebbs and flows,
Our trust, like anchors, always grows.
In moments lost and found anew,
Together, we'll see each journey through.

As tides can rise and oceans swell,
We'll weather storms, and all is well.
For in the depths of every fear,
Our friendship shines, forever clear.

So here we are, come what may,
In tides of friendship, we shall stay.
Through every turn that life may take,
We'll navigate for each other's sake.

Canvas of Companionship

On this canvas, life unfolds,
With every stroke, our story molds.
In colors bright and shades of grace,
Together we paint, each moment's place.

With laughter loud and whispers sweet,
Our masterpiece becomes complete.
In trials faced, in joy we share,
Our bond a treasure, rich and rare.

Each brush of life, a vivid hue,
In canvas vast, it's me and you.
Through storms that rage and skies so clear,
In companionship, we conquer fear.

As seasons change and shadows play,
We'll cherish each and every day.
Together crafting every dream,
In love's embrace, we're a radiant beam.

So let the colors blend and shine,
In this canvas, you are mine.
Through thick and thin, we'll always see,
In the art of life, we are free.

Strength in Shared Currents

In the depths we find our way,
Bound by currents of the day.
Together we rise, together we stand,
With strength that flows, hand in hand.

Through seasons turning, hearts align,
A tapestry of souls entwined.
In whispered dreams, our voices blend,
In unity's embrace, we transcend.

The waves may crash, the storms may blow,
Yet in our hearts, a steady glow.
With courage deep, we face the fight,
Together we shine, a guiding light.

Amidst the strife, we hold the line,
A bond unbroken, fierce and fine.
In shared resolve, we find our might,
Through shadows cast, we seek the light.

So here we stand, a vibrant crew,
In every challenge, we push through.
With strength enshrined in every breath,
We honor life, defying death.

The Voyage of Kindred Souls

Together we sail on open seas,
With hearts aglow in a gentle breeze.
In laughter shared, we chart our course,
With kindred spirits, we find our force.

Each wave that breaks brings tales anew,
Of distant lands and skies so blue.
In harmony, our voices sing,
The journey binds, and hope takes wing.

Through tempests fierce, we steer as one,
In darkest nights, we wait for dawn.
For every storm that tests our bond,
In every trial, we've grown so fond.

Our anchor lies in trust and grace,
In every smile, in every face.
The stars above will guide our way,
In unity, we greet the day.

So let us roam, where dreams unfold,
In every sunset, stories told.
With hearts aligned, we will explore,
The beauty found in kindness' core.

Harboring Heartfelt Support

In quiet moments, warmth surrounds,
A haven safe where love abounds.
With open arms and listening ears,
We navigate through doubts and fears.

When shadows loom, we light the way,
In gentle words, we choose to stay.
With every tear, a bridge is built,
In shared silence, we find our guilt.

We weave our tales of joy and pain,
In every loss, there's much to gain.
With every laugh, a healing song,
In unity, we are so strong.

No need to stand alone in strife,
For here we lift, embrace all life.
With whispered hopes, we mend the heart,
In this safe space, we never part.

So take my hand, let's walk this path,
In every moment, feel the warmth's wrath.
With heartfelt support, we rise anew,
In love's embrace, our spirits grew.

Crafted from Common Experiences

From shared moments, our bond is spun,
In echoes of laughter, we have won.
Through trials faced, our spirits shine,
In every setback, a chance to align.

Together we weave the tapestry bold,
With stories of courage, wisdom told.
In every struggle, a chance to see,
How strength arises from you and me.

In simple joys, we find the thread,
Connecting hearts, where fears have fled.
From whispered dreams to silent screams,
In our unity, hope brightly beams.

So let us gather, let voices rise,
In every challenge, a new surprise.
With laughter shared and tears we shed,
Crafted from life, our spirits are fed.

In every heartbeat, we find our place,
Together we journey, a shared embrace.
For in our stories, we truly grow,
Bound by the love that we both know.

The Voyage of Bonds

Across the sea, our sails unfurl,
With every wave, our dreams entwirl.
The compass points to hearts embraced,
In every storm, a bond is traced.

Through endless nights, the stars our guide,
In whispered winds, love won't subside.
We journey on, two souls as one,
With every dawn, a race begun.

The tide may shift, the skies may roar,
Yet in your eyes, I find the shore.
Our anchors set in trust anew,
Together strong, we break on through.

From distant lands, we share our tales,
With joy in hearts, we set our sails.
Through tempests fierce, our spirits rise,
By love's embrace, we claim the skies.

In every port, our flags will fly,
For bonds of love will never die.
Through voyage grand, forever free,
In every heartbeat, you're with me.

Reflections in the Deep

Beneath the waves, where silence dwells,
A world of secrets, nature tells.
Mirrored dreams on water's skin,
In quiet depths, the heart begins.

Each ripple speaks of stories past,
Of loves once lost and friendships cast.
In the stillness, the soul can see,
The whispered truth that sets us free.

Coral gardens, colors bright,
Where shadows dance in soft twilight.
Emerald fish and currents strong,
In this refuge, we all belong.

As sunbeams filter down so slow,
In tranquil waters, peace will grow.
Reflections gleam like dreams awake,
In depths profound, our hearts will quake.

When storms arise and tides conspire,
We dive beneath, our hearts on fire.
For in the deep, the truth reveals,
The strength of love, the heart that heals.

Shorelines of Serenity

The waves caress the golden shore,
In every breath, I seek for more.
With every tide, my worries fade,
In nature's arms, my fears allayed.

Footprints left on sandy ground,
In solitude, my peace is found.
Seagulls dance and gulls take flight,
In this haven, hearts ignite.

Beneath the sun's warm, gentle rays,
I lose myself in endless days.
The horizon stretches far and wide,
In quiet moments, love's our guide.

With lullabies of ocean's swell,
Each whispered wave casts a spell.
As twilight drapes its velvet cloak,
My heart the ocean's dreams invoke.

In this embrace of earth and sea,
I find my home, I find the key.
For in this space where spirits soar,
The shorelines hold my heart's true core.

Ripple Effects of Love

A gentle touch, a knowing glance,
An echo of a sweet romance.
In every smile, a spark ignites,
Creating waves on starry nights.

Like pebbles dropped in waters clear,
Each act of love draws you near.
With every ripple, hearts combine,
In fluid grace, our souls align.

The subtle strength in simple deeds,
Nurtures roots of tender seeds.
As kindness flows from heart to heart,
The world transforms, we all take part.

Every laugh, each tear we share,
Binds us close with threads of care.
In storms of life, our love will stand,
A lifeline forged by fate's own hand.

So let the ripples spread and swell,
In every story weaves our spell.
For love, like water, knows no end,
In every wave, we greet, we mend.

Lighthouse of Loyalty

In the stormy sea we stand,
Guiding light, a steady hand.
Through the waves and darkest night,
Your presence shines, a beacon bright.

When shadows loom, you are my shield,
In your warmth, my fears are healed.
Together strong, we will not sway,
In the harbor, come what may.

Loyalty's flame, forever true,
In every challenge, me and you.
With open hearts, through thick and thin,
Our voyage starts, let love begin.

A lighthouse standing proud and tall,
With every rise and every fall.
You stand firm, a guiding ray,
In this life, we find our way.

Through time and tide, we'll always stay,
Chasing dreams and light of day.
Oh, steadfast friend, I'll sail with you,
Together, hopes will see us through.

Driftwood of Memories

Waves whisper secrets on the shore,
Driftwood carries tales of yore.
Each piece a story, worn and true,
Fragments of life, me and you.

Gathered treasures from the tide,
Moments cherished, hearts confide.
We build our dreams on sandy ground,
In this dance, our love is found.

With every wave, old ghosts arise,
Reflections caught in ocean's eyes.
Through gentle storms, our bond won't break,
For every memory, love we make.

In the twilight, we'll reminisce,
Holding on to each sweet kiss.
Driftwood scattered, yet we see,
The beauty found in you and me.

The tides of life will ebb and flow,
But our love will only grow.
From driftwood's heart, we'll weave our dreams,
In every wave, our future gleams.

Navigating Through Shared Dreams

In the twilight, stars align,
Two souls merge, your hand in mine.
With every heartbeat, we embark,
Navigating through the dark.

Our dreams like constellations gleam,
Guiding paths through night's deep stream.
Together, charts and maps we draw,
In this journey, we find our law.

Bound by visions, futures bright,
We chase the dawn, embracing light.
In whispered hopes, our spirits soar,
Finding treasures on distant shores.

Through storms that test, we won't divide,
With anchor strong, you're by my side.
In every venture, we are found,
With love's compass, we are bound.

The winds may change, but we will sail,
Together, facing every gale.
In soothing waves, our dreams unite,
Navigating through the night.

Tethered by Time

In moments fleeting, we hold tight,
Tethered by love, a gentle light.
As seasons change, our roots run deep,
In memories shared, our hearts will keep.

Through sunlit days and starry skies,
In laughter shared, where solace lies.
With every tick of the clock's hand,
We weave our bond, a timeless strand.

For every sorrow, joys we find,
Life's tender hold, forever kind.
In quiet whispers and soft embrace,
With every breath, we find our place.

As years may pass, and shadows grow,
Together still, we'll face the flow.
Tethered in time, your heart, my guide,
In every moment, side by side.

With unified steps, through life's grand race,
Memories made, a cherished space.
In love's embrace, forever we climb,
Eternally bound, tethered by time.

Anchors of Affection

In turbulent seas, you hold me tight,
Your love, my anchor in the night.
When waves crash down, I find my way,
With you beside me, I'll never sway.

Through storms that threaten, we endure,
In every struggle, we find the cure.
Your gentle strength, my soft repose,
In deep waters where affection grows.

Time may erode the softest sand,
But our bond stands, forever grand.
Through shifting tides, we shall remain,
In this harbor, we feel no pain.

Life's tempest rises, yet still we stand,
With anchors of affection, hand in hand.
In every challenge, our love will rise,
In sacred whispers, beneath the skies.

Beyond horizons, we carve our path,
In each embrace, we share the wrath.
So let the waves crash, loud and free,
Together, my love, it's you and me.

Currents of Connection

Beneath the surface, currents flow,
Invisible ties we come to know.
With every glance, a bridge we build,
In silent whispers, our hearts are thrilled.

As time unwinds, our souls entwine,
In gentle pulses, love's design.
Through every tide, we feel the pull,
In currents strong, our hearts are full.

Shared laughter dances on the breeze,
Time becomes a stream, a tease.
In waves of joy, we lose our place,
But find each other, warm embrace.

Moments drift like leaves in fall,
Yet still, we rise, we never stall.
Through swirling eddies, we are found,
In blessed waters, love is crowned.

In every journey, hand in hand,
We embrace the flow, a sacred plan.
Together we navigate the sea,
In currents of connection, just you and me.

The Vast Expanse of Reunion

In the soft glow of twilight's embrace,
Old friends gather, faces aglow.
Laughter dances like fireflies,
Time weaves tales in gentle flow.

Stories shared beneath the stars,
Echoing joys and bittersweet pain.
Hearts reconnect, like rivers to seas,
In the vast expanse, love will remain.

Memories glimmer in the night air,
A tapestry woven so fine.
With every hug, a promise made,
In this sacred space, we intertwine.

Every moment a treasure, a gift,
In the warmth of familiar hands.
Together, we stand, together we shift,
Uniting as life's journey expands.

As dawn approaches with soft sighs,
We bid farewell, yet not apart.
For in every heart, a piece resides,
The vast expanse, our love's true art.

Navigators of Nuance

In the currents of thought, we sail,
Each whisper a breeze, a guiding hand.
Through waters deep and uncharted trails,
Navigators of nuance, we make our stand.

With colors of minds that shimmer bright,
Each perspective a star on the sea.
Together we chart through day and night,
Finding the beauty in what we can't see.

A canvas of voices, each tone unique,
Painting the world with rich diversions.
In this dance of dialogue, we seek,
To bridge our differences, heal the conversions.

As waves crash softly, we'll make our way,
With compassion our compass, hearts ablaze.
Together we'll journey, come what may,
Navigators of nuance, through life's maze.

In the stillness, listen to the song,
Of all that connects us, voices entwined.
For we are stronger, not just along,
But in the depths of understanding defined.

Riding the Swells of Support

On turbulent seas, we find our place,
Riding the swells that rise and fall.
With arms outstretched, we embrace,
United in courage, answering the call.

Through storms we weather, side by side,
Hearts bolstered by friendship's light.
In moments of doubt, we will abide,
Lifting each other, soaring in flight.

Together we anchor when shadows creep,
Casting aside our worries and fears.
With laughter and love, our spirits leap,
Creating a bond that forever endears.

As tides may shift, we stand as one,
Navigating life's ebb and flow.
With every trial, our strength is spun,
In the sea of support, we shall grow.

With the stars as our guide, we sail ahead,
Embracing the waves, our hearts stay true.
Riding the swells, where love is spread,
In the journey together, me and you.

Echoes Across the Waters

In the quiet dusk of falling light,
Echoes ripple across the lake.
Whispers of dreams take graceful flight,
Carried by winds that gently wake.

Reflections dance on the water's face,
Each wave a story, old yet new.
In every splash, a trace of grace,
Connections formed in the morning dew.

Voices blend in the tranquil air,
Melodies drifting like soft sighs.
In the embrace of the sun's last glare,
Friendships bloom, where memories rise.

As shadows stretch with the day's retreat,
We gather the moments that softly gleam.
Echoes across, like heartbeats meet,
In the stillness, we weave our dream.

Together we stand, hands intertwined,
In the cool embrace of twilight's glow.
Across the waters, our hearts aligned,
Echoes of love in the afterflow.

The Navigational Star of Friendship

In the night sky, bright and clear,
A guiding star that draws us near.
Through storms and trials, we hold tight,
Together we shine, a beacon of light.

With laughter shared and secrets told,
We weave a bond that won't grow cold.
In each other's eyes, we find our ease,
A treasure trove of memories.

When paths diverge, we still remain,
In heart and spirit, free from pain.
The joy of friendship knows no end,
Forevermore, we shall transcend.

Through every journey, side by side,
Our navigational star, our pride.
In unity, we rise and soar,
With every laughter, we explore.

As seasons change and days grow old,
The stories shared are purest gold.
With every moment, bonds will bloom,
Our friendship lights the darkest room.

Stitching the Fabric of Together

In threads of kindness, we entwine,
A tapestry rich, where hearts align.
With every stitch, we craft our fate,
Together we rise, it's never late.

Each color vibrant, each pattern bold,
Stories woven, both new and old.
In laughter's echo, in joy's embrace,
The fabric of life, a sacred space.

With patience strong, we mend the tears,
In moments shared, we cast our cares.
From joy to sorrow, we all partake,
Creating a quilt from every ache.

The seams may fray, but still we hold,
A bond unbreakable, a story told.
In every corner, a love displayed,
Our patchwork heart, forever made.

As time rolls on and fabrics fade,
We cherish the memories we have laid.
For in this weaving, we find our worth,
Stitching the fabric, a love rebirth.

The Tapestry of Togetherness

In every thread, a story spun,
A tapestry bright, where two are one.
We create beauty with every fold,
Together we share, brave and bold.

With each new color, a dream we chase,
United in purpose, in endless grace.
In laughter's hue and struggle's grind,
Together we flourish, our hearts aligned.

Woven through moments, both thick and thin,
A bond unbreakable, deep within.
Though seasons change, and patterns shift,
Our tapestry remains, a timeless gift.

In woven warmth, we find our peace,
In sharing lives, our joys increase.
With every knot, our strength will show,
The tapestry of love will grow.

In every gathering, every cheer,
The fabric of togetherness draws near.
Through trials met and joys we share,
Our tapestry blooms, beyond compare.

Ocean of Shared Hearts

In oceans deep, where dreams reside,
We sail together, side by side.
With waves of laughter, tides of grace,
Our hearts set forth in a boundless space.

The sun will rise, the stars will gleam,
In every current, we chase a dream.
In storms we face, we find our strength,
Navigating life at every length.

With shores of kindness on which we stand,
Hand in hand, we'll roam this land.
The treasures found in shared embrace,
In this vast ocean, we find our place.

Each wave that crashes, a story told,
In tides of love, our hearts enfold.
Together we dive, unafraid to sink,
In depths of trust, we find our link.

As sunsets fade on waters wide,
We journey forth, with hope as our guide.
In the ocean of shared hearts, we thrive,
Forever together, we will survive.

Navigating the Depths of Affection

In silence deep, our hearts do dwell,
Waves of warmth, like a gentle swell.
Yearning glances, soft and bright,
Guiding us through the endless night.

With every touch, affection grows,
Roots entwined where the wild wind blows.
In tender whispers, secrets share,
Navigating depths, our souls laid bare.

Through laughter bright and tears uncried,
A compass forged in love, we bide.
Echoes of dreams in a vast expanse,
Together we rise, a sweet romance.

The tide may pull, but we hold tight,
In shadowed waters, we find our light.
Sailing forth, in stormy seas,
Navigating depths, we find our ease.

With every heartbeat, we take flight,
In the warmth of love's pure light.
Together, through the waves we bond,
In the depths of affection, forever fond.

Embracing the Gales of Care

Against the winds, we stand so strong,
In the heart of storms, where we belong.
Gentle hands, a sturdy tether,
Embracing gales that bind us together.

A tempest roars, but we remain,
In whispered hopes, we ease the pain.
With every laughter, we start anew,
Finding comfort in the bond so true.

Through swirling skies, our spirits soar,
In winds of change, we seek the core.
A dance of trust, a graceful stride,
Embracing gales, where love won't hide.

Together we weather the fiercest night,
In the eye of the storm, we find our light.
With wings of care, we rise above,
In the tempest's heart, there lives our love.

Though skies may darken, we won't despair,
In every gale, we choose to care.
Together we'll sail to brighter shores,
Embracing gales, forever yours.

Our Voyage, Our Choices

With every tide, we chart our way,
In life's great sea, come what may.
Our hearts set sail on paths unknown,
Together bound, never alone.

From fleeting dreams to visions vast,
In every choice, our anchors cast.
Through sunlight's glow and shadows thrown,
Our voyage leads, as seeds are sown.

Each wave a lesson, each storm a guide,
In trust we flourish, side by side.
Navigating moments, both true and wild,
In every journey, love reconciled.

The stars above, our beacons bright,
Illuminate the depths of night.
With joy we sail, through calm and strife,
Our voyage we honor, this dance of life.

With open hearts, we brave the sea,
In every choice, we choose to be.
Hand in hand, we chart our course,
Together forever, love is the force.

Bonds that Weather the Storm

In raging winds, we're tried and tested,
Through turbulent times, love's manifested.
With steadfast hearts that beat in rhyme,
Bonds that weather, through space and time.

Each drop of rain, a tale retold,
In shared embraces, warmth unfolds.
With laughter echoing, fears disarm,
In arms entwined, we face the harm.

Through trials faced, our spirits rise,
In the heart of storms, we find the prize.
With every challenge that we withstand,
United forever, together we stand.

No tempest fierce could break our tie,
In every moment, you and I.
With unwavering trust, we hold so near,
Bonds that weather, a love sincere.

As clouds disperse, the sunlight streams,
Woven in courage, we chase our dreams.
Through every tempest, we'll remain strong,
Our bonds unyielding, our hearts a song.

Sailing on Trust's Sea

We set our sails on a bright blue tide,
Waves of hope where dreams abide.
With every gust, our worries cease,
In each other, we find our peace.

The stars above are our guiding lights,
Navigating through the stormy nights.
With hearts aligned and spirits free,
We drift along Trust's endless sea.

Anchored in faith, we find our way,
Turning the dark into dawn's new day.
Together we chart our course anew,
In unity, there's nothing we can't do.

As the sun sets, we whisper dreams,
In the quiet, our laughter beams.
With every tide, we rise and fall,
But anchored in trust, we stand tall.

So raise your glass to the journey ahead,
To the uncharted paths we've boldly tread.
With trust as our compass, we shall not stray,
Sailing on Trust's sea, come what may.

In the Heart's Harbor

In the heart's harbor, where love anchors deep,
Waves of emotion, secrets we keep.
Sheltering dreams, our spirits entwined,
In this safe place, our souls are aligned.

The gentle breeze carries whispers of care,
In the stillness, our laughter fills air.
With every heartbeat, we build a home,
In the heart's harbor, we are never alone.

Through storms and shadows, we'll stand side by side,
In the warmth of each other, we'll always confide.
With each passing tide, our bonds will grow strong,
In love's embrace, we will always belong.

As dusk paints the sky with hues of gold,
We share our stories, the new and the old.
In the heart's harbor, our fears fade away,
Guided by love, we'll find our way.

So let the waves crash, let the winds blow,
With faith in each other, we'll navigate flow.
In the heart's harbor, our dreams will ignite,
Together forever, in love's pure light.

Weaving Together Moments

In the tapestry of time, we craft our song,
Each thread a memory where we belong.
With laughter and tears, we stitch day by day,
Weaving together moments that forever stay.

A patch of joy, a swirl of grace,
In this quilt of life, we find our place.
With love as our loom, we intertwine,
Creating a masterpiece, yours and mine.

Through seasons that change, our fabric holds tight,
In every sunrise, we breathe in the light.
With every heartbeat, each moment we share,
Weaving together, life's delicate care.

As colors blend in this vibrant scene,
The threads of our lives, a beautiful sheen.
With patience and love, in every embrace,
We create a legacy, our timeless grace.

So let's dance through the years, hand in hand,
In this woven journey, together we stand.
With every stitch, our story unfolds,
Weaving together moments, worth more than gold.

Under the Canopy of Kinship

Beneath the branches where memories sway,
Under the canopy, we find our way.
In the shade of love, our hearts convene,
Creating a bond, strong and serene.

Through laughter and stories, our roots intertwine,
In the warmth of kinship, our spirits align.
With every twist, our family tree grows,
In unity, we stand against life's throes.

With gentle whispers and hands held tight,
We navigate darkness, embracing the light.
Under this canopy, together we dream,
Finding our strength in love's endless theme.

Through seasons of change, we weather the storms,
In the shelter of kinship, our hearts stay warm.
As leaves fall and blossom, we cherish it all,
Under the canopy, we'll never fall.

So gather around, let's celebrate now,
In the embrace of our roots, take a bow.
For under this canopy, together we'll thrive,
In the beauty of kinship, we come alive.

Beyond the Horizon of Understanding

In distant realms, where whispers fade,
Truths entwine like shadows played.
We reach for stars, yet grasp the air,
Beyond horizons, dreams laid bare.

Each thought a wave, a cresting tide,
Waves of knowledge, far and wide.
Yet silence lingers, speaks so loud,
In understanding, we are proud.

With open hearts, we take the leap,
Into the depths, where thoughts run deep.
Unraveling knots of fear and doubt,
Together, we will find the route.

Each journey starts with one bold step,
Through valleys vast, where echoes prep.
Hold on to hope, let kindness reign,
In unity, we break the chain.

So sail with me beyond the night,
In search of truth, for it is right.
Together, we will find the way,
Beyond horizons, come what may.

The Ocean of Empathy

Beneath the waves, a current flows,
Through depths of heart, a kindness grows.
We dip our toes in waters wide,
In this ocean, we must abide.

A gentle touch can soothe the soul,
Like softest waves that make us whole.
With every splash, we learn to care,
In empathy, we find our share.

Droplets dance on open seas,
Carrying whispers on the breeze.
We lend an ear, we share a tear,
In this ocean, we conquer fear.

Not just the surface, but depths profound,
In every heart, let love be found.
Together we swim, hand in hand,
In unity, we make our stand.

So cast your cares upon the tide,
In this ocean, let love reside.
Each wave a bond, each tide a thread,
In the ocean of empathy, we're fed.

Charting the Course of Care

With maps unrolled and compass true,
We trace the paths that guide us through.
Each line a promise, each word a spark,
In the dark waters, we find our mark.

Through storms that roar and skies that weep,
Our hearts will navigate, bold and deep.
With every choice, a beacon shines,
In the course of care, love entwines.

The stars above, our steadfast guide,
Illuminate the waves with pride.
In gentle winds, we learn to steer,
Charting a course that draws us near.

Through rocky shores and tempestuous tides,
We hold each other, where trust abides.
Fueled by hope, we journey far,
In the course of care, we are the stars.

So let us sail with grace and ease,
Across the seas, through moments seized.
Together, as one, we will declare,
The strength that flows in hearts that care.

Crosswinds of Communication

In every word, a breeze is felt,
A gentle gust, where feelings melt.
We share our thoughts, both near and far,
In crosswinds' dance, we are who we are.

The whispers float like leaves in air,
A tapestry of voices rare.
With open hearts, we find our sound,
In communication, bonds are found.

As clouds converge, the storms may rise,
Yet clarity shines through cloudy skies.
In every challenge, lessons bloom,
From crosswinds' strength, we chase the gloom.

With each exchange, a bridge is built,
Untangling fears, dissolving guilt.
On currents strong, we navigate,
In crosswinds of love, we cultivate.

So let your voice soar high and free,
Embrace the winds, just you and me.
In this chorus, let harmony sing,
Where crosswinds of communication bring.

Navigate by Laughter

In the breeze of joy we sail,
With laughter as our guiding trail.
The waves of cheer, they lift us high,
Together, we chase the endless sky.

With every chuckle, we find our way,
Through stormy nights and sunny day.
We dance on decks of playful glee,
Navigating life, just you and me.

A compass made of friendship true,
Our hearts, a map; our dreams, the blue.
In laughter's warmth, we weather strife,
Sailing onward, hand in hand for life.

Every joke and every jest,
In laughter's realm, we feel our best.
As waves may crash, our spirits shine,
Together we thrive, our paths align.

So here we are, in mirth entwined,
With laughter's light, our souls combined.
Navigating through both calm and storm,
In our hearts, love keeps us warm.

Tides of Togetherness

The tides roll in, a rhythm sweet,
With every wave, our hearts do meet.
A shore of friendship, strong and true,
We face each dawn, just me and you.

Together we stand on sandy ground,
In the whispers of waves, our joys abound.
With laughter shared and hands held tight,
We weather the day, we embrace the night.

The moonlight dances on ocean's crest,
Bringing calm to hearts at rest.
In the warmth of waves, we make our mark,
This bond we have ignites a spark.

As the tides may ebb and flow with grace,
Together we find our special place.
For in the currents of life we flow,
Side by side, through highs and lows.

And when the storms may rage and roar,
We find our shelter on that shore.
With every tide, our bond grows strong,
In this journey together, we belong.

Canvas of Companionship

On a canvas wide, we brush our dreams,
With colors bright, and flowing streams.
A palette rich with laughter's hue,
Each stroke a memory, just me and you.

In every line, our stories blend,
A masterpiece, where hearts transcend.
With gentle shades of warmth and care,
A tapestry woven, beyond compare.

As the seasons shift and colors fade,
Together we paint, never afraid.
With the brush of trust, we create with zeal,
In this art of life, our hearts reveal.

In every canvas, challenges await,
Yet united, we celebrate.
For in the creation, we find our place,
Each moment shared, a stroke of grace.

So let us gather 'neath the stars at night,
With dreams and hopes, our futures bright.
In this canvas of companionship, we thrive,
Together in art, we come alive.

Harbors of Affection

In the harbor's glow, affection's light,
We anchor dreams and hold them tight.
With open arms, we greet the day,
In the safety found, we long to stay.

The waves may crash; the winds may wail,
Yet love's soft whispers always prevail.
In this sanctuary, our hearts find home,
Through storms of life, we will not roam.

With lanterns lit, we share our fears,
In silent nights, we dry our tears.
With every heartbeat, we build our shelter,
In harbors of love, we grow together.

As tides may change, and sunsets fades,
We trace our paths, in love's charades.
Through every challenge, side by side,
In the arms of affection, we abide.

So let the waves crash, let the winds blow,
In these harbors of affection, our hearts will grow.
Together we weather whatever may come,
In our haven of love, we are forever home.

Windward Wishes

Upon the breeze, whispers soft,
Scattered hopes aloft,
In the gentle sway of trees,
Hearts dance in the ease.

A sailor's song, the stars ignite,
Guiding dreams through night,
With every gust, a wish takes flight,
Chasing dawn's light.

Clouds drift like thoughts, ever free,
Carried across the sea,
In the embrace of the wind's caress,
Nature's sweet finesse.

Wandering hearts find solace here,
In whispers, they draw near,
With each echo of the gale,
Their stories set sail.

Bound by tides, we share our fate,
The ocean's heart resonates,
Together in the currents' sway,
We find our way.

The Current of Kinship

In the flow, we intertwine,
Connected by a line,
Every wave, a tale unfolds,
A warmth in the cold.

Shared laughter rides the tide,
In this bond, we confide,
Moments drift, yet they remain,
Love's gentle refrain.

Though storms may come, we stand strong,
Together, we belong,
Holding tight through waves of change,
In currents, we rearrange.

Roots deep like ancient trees,
In the wind, our stories tease,
Every ebb, a reminder clear,
Of those we hold dear.

With each rise, we breathe anew,
In this bond, ever true,
Flowing forward, hand in hand,
Together, we withstand.

Driftwood Dreams

On sandy shores where shadows play,
Driftwood whispers of yesterday,
Carried forth by the restless tide,
In salty tales, our hopes reside.

Pieces of time, worn and blessed,
Each tell a story, a silent quest,
In fragile grace, they find their way,
To shores where memories stay.

Beneath the moon's soft silvery glow,
The dreams of wanderers begin to flow,
As tides retreat, so do we dare,
To weave new dreams upon the air.

We gather the fragments, the pieces we find,
In this gathering, hearts relearn to bind,
With each gentle wave, a spark ignites,
To light our souls on endless nights.

A tapestry forged from tales unsaid,
In driftwood whispers, our paths are led,
And with the dawn, as we chase the light,
We hold our dreams, forever in flight.

Nautical Narratives of Us

With sails unfurled, we chart a course,
Through storms and calm, we feel the force,
In every wave, a story starts,
Nautical journeys warm our hearts.

Anchored deep in trust and grace,
In the tides, we find our place,
Every sunrise, a promise made,
In every breeze, our fears shall fade.

From shores unknown, we venture wide,
With compass set and hearts as guide,
Through oceans vast, we share our dreams,
In salty air, our laughter gleams.

Weaving tales in moonlit nights,
By starlit skies, our spirits take flight,
The echoes of our shared embrace,
In nautical tales, we find our grace.

As waves recede, new journeys call,
Together, we will face them all,
In the heart of the sea, where stories draw,
Our love, an everlasting law.

Driftwood of Kindred Spirits

Waves whisper secrets in the night,
Driftwood carries tales of flight.
Bound by the currents, hearts align,
Together we rise, as stars entwine.

Roots of friendship, tangle and weave,
In the soft sands, we dare believe.
Each piece of wood, a story told,
In storms we flourish, in sun we hold.

We gather each fragment, piece by piece,
From distant shores, we find our peace.
Kindred spirits on the tides we roam,
In the ocean's embrace, we find our home.

Light flickers gently, guiding our way,
Through tempest's fury, we choose to stay.
Together we dance, in shadows and light,
Driftwood of dreams, our spirits take flight.

So here's to the journey, our paths intertwined,
In the waves of fate, our souls aligned.
With each ebb and flow, forever we'll sing,
Driftwood of kindred, in unity, we bring.

Sailing into New Tomorrows

Anchors lifted, sails unfurled,
Chasing horizons, a brand new world.
With wind in our hearts, we steer the day,
Sailing into tomorrows, come what may.

Stars above us, a guiding light,
Through darkest waters, we hold on tight.
Every wave whispers a tale anew,
Painting our dreams in vibrant hues.

Breath of the ocean, sweet and free,
Unraveling the knots of destiny.
Together we voyage, hand in hand,
Plotting our course through uncharted land.

With every sunrise, hope is reborn,
A canvas awaits, our spirits adorn.
In laughter and joy, in trials we face,
Sailing into new tomorrows, we embrace.

As seagulls dance, we lift our eyes,
To infinite places beneath endless skies.
In unity's arc, we find our sway,
Sailing into new tomorrows, come what may.

Comrades Across the Abyss

Echoes of courage, call through the dark,
Comrades beside me, we ignite a spark.
Facing the shadows that loom and creep,
Together we'll manage the depths of the deep.

With battle cries ringing, our voices blend,
In this vast abyss, we rise and defend.
Every heartbeat, a promise made,
In the silence of struggle, we will not fade.

Hand in hand, we traverse the night,
In the heart of the storm, we find our light.
For every trial, a bond will grow,
Comrades across the abyss, we'll always know.

Through time and passage, our spirits will soar,
United in purpose, forever we'll explore.
Amongst the chaos, our hearts align,
Comrades across the abyss, forever we shine.

So let the winds howl, let the tempests rage,
We stand together, turning the page.
In the depths of despair, in love's sweet kiss,
Comrades across the abyss, we find our bliss.

Captains of Companionship

Navigating waters, both calm and wild,
Captains of companionship, sweetly styled.
With maps of laughter and compass of dreams,
Together we sail on life's flowing streams.

Every storm faced, we anchor so tight,
Guided through darkness, we follow the light.
In the quiet moments, our hearts feel the call,
Captains together, we conquer it all.

With the wind at our backs, we journey forth,
Explorers of love, seeking true worth.
Through the waves of time, our bonds will grow,
Captains of companionship, ready to flow.

In the sunsets glowing, we find our peace,
Our ship of memories will never cease.
As stars guide our path, in a sky full of dreams,
Together as captains, we craft our themes.

So here's to the voyages, the tales yet to live,
To love that we share, all that we give.
On this endless ocean, together we roam,
Captains of companionship, we've found our home.

The Nautical Ties that Bind

In the harbor where dreams collide,
Each vessel holds a tale inside.
With every wave, we learn to glide,
Together, on this eager tide.

Beneath the stars, we find our way,
Navigating night and day.
With sturdy ropes, our fears allayed,
In friendship's light, we choose to stay.

The sailor's chant, a sweet refrain,
Echoes softly through the rain.
In laughter shared, we ease the pain,
Our souls entwined, none left in vain.

A compass points to one another,
We are sisters, we are brothers.
Through storms of life, we seek to tether,
In unity, we brave the weather.

Bound by ties that weather time,
Our spirits soar, our hearts in rhyme.
In every port, a chance to climb,
Together, we are boundless prime.

Sails of Shared Struggles

Raise the sails, let courage fly,
With every gust, we reach the sky.
In shared struggles, we reply,
Building dreams as days go by.

When clouds gather and shadows loom,
We stand together, face the gloom.
With steady hearts, we find a room,
In brotherhood, we swiftly zoom.

Each stitch in canvas tells our tale,
In unity, we shall prevail.
Through troubled seas, we will not bail,
With hope's soft light, we set our sail.

Our laughter rings across the sea,
In every wave, we find the key.
With open hearts, we hold the spree,
Together strong, we'll always be.

So lift your voice and take a stand,
In every port, we'll make a band.
With sails of struggle, hand in hand,
We navigate this vast, wide land.

Untangling Life's Ropes

Life's tangled ropes can weigh us down,
But in their knots, we'll wear a crown.
Through each twist, we find our sound,
In unity, our strength is found.

With gentle hands, we pry apart,
Each binding loop a work of art.
For every end, there's a new start,
Together, we mend every heart.

In the mess, there lies a chance,
To weave together our own dance.
With every step, we take a stance,
In life's great sea, we choose romance.

Through shared trials, we grow wise,
In laughter shared, the darkness flies.
With every bridge, new paths arise,
United, we reach for the skies.

So trust the ties that interlace,
In every hug, let love embrace.
With open arms, we find our place,
Together, life's a wondrous race.

Journey of the Linked Hearts

On this journey, hand in hand,
Together, we will bravely stand.
Through winding paths, where dreams expand,
In every beat, our joys are planned.

As seasons change, we feel the breeze,
In every moment, find the keys.
With every laugh, we climb the trees,
In linked hearts, we find our ease.

Through valleys low and mountains high,
With tireless spirits, we will fly.
In whispers soft, our dreams comply,
Forever shining, like the sky.

Our journey's map is drawn in song,
With tales of love where we belong.
In every note, we are thus strong,
Together singing all night long.

So hold my hand, let's pave a way,
In every challenge, come what may.
With linked hearts, we'll seize the day,
Forever bound, come what may.

Rafts of Resilience

In rising tides, we learn to float,
With sturdy hearts, we stay remote.
Through storms that rage, we hold on tight,
Together we find our way to light.

When winds howl fierce, and shadows creep,
Our faith runs deep, our dreams we keep.
On rafts of hope, we navigate,
With every challenge, we elevate.

Each wave a test, each splash a trial,
Yet through it all, we wear a smile.
United we stand, we will not break,
In our shared strength, new paths we make.

Beneath the stars, our spirits soar,
In the darkest nights, we will explore.
The journey long, but hearts embrace,
Resilience shines in every space.

So raise your sails, let courage rise,
In every setback, new hope lies.
Together we'll conquer the raging sea,
On rafts of resilience, we are free.

Echoes of Laughter

In a sunlit park, our voices blend,
With joy unbound, our hearts we send.
Each chuckle shared, a bond so bright,
Echoes of laughter, pure delight.

Through playful games, we dance and sway,
In gentle breezes, worries stray.
With every joke, our spirits lift,
These cherished moments, the greatest gift.

Around the fire, as stories flow,
In flickering light, our memories glow.
A tapestry woven with threads of cheer,
Echoes of laughter, forever near.

In times of trouble, we find our way,
With humor's spark, we're led to play.
For laughter shared is love expressed,
In each warm smile, we are blessed.

So gather close, let the joy arise,
In echoes of laughter, our spirits rise.
Through every season, hand in hand,
Together we shine, a joyous band.

Kites Flying in Harmony

In open fields where soft winds blow,
Kites soaring high, putting on a show.
Colors unite in the bright blue sky,
Dancing together, they gracefully fly.

With each tug and pull of the string to hold,
A ballet of friendship, a story told.
In laughter and joy, our spirits intertwine,
Kites flying high, a love divine.

They dip and spin, so wild, so free,
Each twist a lesson in unity.
Through gusts of air, they find their way,
Kites flying together, come what may.

As day fades softly and colors dim,
We watch them glide, horizons brim.
In the fading light, dreams take flight,
Kites flying in harmony, pure delight.

So let us rise, like those kites above,
In gentle breezes, we find our love.
With every ascent, our hearts align,
Kites flying in harmony, forever shine.

Sailboats of Shared Secrets

In the still of night, beneath the stars,
Sailboats drift softly, near and far.
Each whisper shared, a journey starts,
Secrets afloat, entwined in hearts.

Through moonlit waves, we sail and dream,
Symbols of trust in the silver beam.
With every tide, our stories flow,
Sailboats of secrets, together we row.

In the gentle hush, our voices blend,
Trusting the breeze, we tend and mend.
With laughter and sighs, we chart our course,
Sailboats of shared secrets, a tranquil force.

When storms approach, as shadows loom,
In unity, we dispel the gloom.
Together we navigate, hand in hand,
Sailboats of secrets, a steadfast band.

So let us drift through the night's embrace,
With every secret, we find our place.
In the dance of the waves, our dreams ignite,
Sailboats of shared secrets, our guiding light.

Boundless Horizons

In the dawn of day, we rise anew,
Chasing dreams that stretch the sky so blue.
Mountains high and valleys low,
Every step, our spirits grow.

Waves of hope crash on the shore,
Guiding us to seek and explore.
With every breath, the world expands,
Boundless horizons at our hands.

The wind whispers secrets of the day,
Inviting us to find our way.
Through valleys deep and peaks so grand,
Together, we will make our stand.

Stars above, a map of light,
Leading us through the darkest night.
In this journey, side by side,
With boundless hearts, we'll never hide.

So let us dance upon the breeze,
Embrace the moments that we seize.
For in this life, our hopes converge,
On boundless horizons, we emerge.

Uncharted Waters of Trust

In the vessel of our dreams, we sail,
Through uncharted waters, we shall prevail.
With every wave, our courage tests,
In the heart of adventure, our spirit rests.

The compass guides us through the night,
Trusting each other, we find our light.
Amid the storms that fiercely blow,
Together, we will learn and grow.

With sails unfurled, we chase the dawn,
In this vast ocean, we are reborn.
Cautious whispers in the dark,
Build faith in each little spark.

The tides may shift, the winds may change,
But our bond remains uninjured, strange.
Through the waves of doubt and fear,
We shall navigate, knowing love is near.

So let us journey, hearts aligned,
Through uncharted waters, fate defined.
In the depths of trust, we'll always find,
A treasure of memories intertwined.

Beyond the Anchor

In the stillness of the dawn's embrace,
We shed the chains that time won't trace.
Beyond the anchor, our spirits soar,
To places we've yet to explore.

With the horizon as our guide,
We'll let go of fear and pride.
Through open seas, we'll chase the sun,
In every heartbeat, a new begun.

The anchor's weight, a distant past,
As we sail forth, our dreams amassed.
With every wave, new colors blend,
In the journey, we find no end.

Stars will dance upon the tide,
In the depths, we'll learn to glide.
Each moment cherished, never meek,
Beyond the anchor, our souls will speak.

So raise the sails, let winds take flight,
In the vast unknown, we ignite our light.
With every turn and rippling wave,
Beyond the anchor, we are brave.

The Map of Us

In the quiet spaces of our hearts,
Lies a treasure map, where love starts.
Each line drawn tells our story true,
A path laid out for me and you.

Mountains climbed, valleys crossed,
In the journey, never lost.
Every moment, a guiding star,
In the map of us, we'll go far.

Across the rivers, wide and deep,
In this adventure, forever we leap.
With every step, our bond secure,
In the map of us, we endure.

Through forests dense, and skies so clear,
Hand in hand, we conquer fear.
Together, we'll forge our way ahead,
In the map of us, hope is bred.

So here we stand, with hearts so bold,
A love story waiting to be told.
With each page turned, a journey begins,
In the map of us, our love wins.

Threads Tied in Trust

In the fabric of silence, we weave,
Golden threads of moments we believe.
Stitches forged through laughter and tears,
Holding tight through the passing years.

Woven hearts with patterns unique,
In this tapestry, we gently speak.
Each knot a promise, steadfast, sure,
A bond unbroken, forever pure.

Underneath the stars, we thread the night,
Creating patterns that shimmer bright.
Our hands intertwined, a silent guide,
Through every ebb, through every tide.

In the daylight's warmth, our trust is sewn,
A quilt of love that we have grown.
Our stories told in colors bold,
In every thread, a tale unfolds.

Thus, in this trust, we find our way,
Two souls entwined, come what may.
In the moments shared, we shall find,
The threads of trust, forever bind.

Navigating Heartstrings

With gentle hands, we play the strings,
Creating melodies that love brings.
Soft notes of kindness fill the air,
We navigate through joys and cares.

Harmonies that dance upon the breeze,
In every whisper, you make me cease.
A symphony of heart and mind,
In every chord, our fates aligned.

Through valleys deep, and mountains high,
We hear the music of our sighs.
And every chord we choose to play,
Is a step towards a brighter day.

Navigating paths both rough and smooth,
In the rhythm of love, we find our groove.
With every heartstring's gentle pull,
We weave a tapestry, beautiful.

So let us dance to this sweet refrain,
Through storms and calm, through joy and pain.
Together, we will always chart,
The melody that lives in our heart.

Horizon of Hearts

Beyond the sunset, where dreams collide,
The horizon calls, where hopes reside.
In every color that paints the sky,
A whisper of love that will never die.

With every dawn, our spirits rise,
Reaching for stars that fill our eyes.
In the quiet moments, hand in hand,
We explore the shores of this promised land.

Through valleys low and mountains tall,
The horizon beckons, we heed its call.
Together we wander, side by side,
In this journey, we take pride.

Each heartbeat echoes the tales we've spun,
Under the warmth of the shining sun.
With each sunset, we find our way,
Guided by love, day after day.

So here we stand, looking afar,
With dreams woven into every star.
The horizon of hearts, our guiding light,
In the tapestry of love, forever bright.

Ripples of Reciprocity

Drop a thought, watch it spread,
Ripples of kindness, easily said.
In every action, a wave cascades,
Returning to us in lovely shades.

With gentle gestures, we create,
A cycle of love, we cultivate.
In giving and sharing, we find our way,
The joy of reciprocity at play.

Each smile a pebble cast in grace,
Creating ripples that time won't erase.
Through laughter shared and tears we shed,
The ties that bind us are gently spread.

In the quiet moments, let's pause and see,
The magic of giving, the heart's decree.
For every kindness that we express,
Is a seed of hope in the universe.

So let us weave this dance of care,
In the wealth of hearts, a treasure rare.
Through ripples that echo through time and space,
We build a world, a warm embrace.

9 789916 866955